Praise for
LEAVE COMPROMISE *at Home*

I have held numerous leadership positions for much of my adult life. During my tenure in those positions including Chairman of the Board of Trustees at Mt Carmel Baptist Church, as well as their Director of Youth Ministries, and presently as Executive Director of Nepperhan Community Center in Yonkers, New York. I have always found occasion in devising a plan or strategy to have a Plan B or backup plan. However, after reading Leave Compromise At Home, it has given me a fresh outlook on compromise and/or settling for a Plan B. Reginald L. Hudson has carefully and very skillfully challenged our thought process as it relates to the detrimental effects of compromise. I would strongly encourage all who are in or considering leadership to read this book. It will bless you as it has me, and you will never think the same way again in preparing for the future of your family, home, church, business, education, spiritual growth, or your life in general.

Reggie, you have blessed us once again!

Jim Bostic,
Your Brother in Christ

Leave Compromise At Home is a parody with a purpose. Although cute in its storyline, the message is impactful when embraced. If left unaddressed, compromise can lead to the failure of achieving goals and dreams. Compromise encourages you to settle and not exceed.

As you read the pages which follow, reflect on areas in your life where you've compromised and gone for the three point field goal rather than pursuing the six point touchdown. Whatever you do, don't become discouraged, look at where you are and where you desire to be, make your Plan A, then pursue and without fail recover all. Remember, at all cost you want to Leave *Compromise* At Home!

Enjoy and be blessed!

Stephanie L. Quarles, CEO
Healed Hearts, Inc.

LEAVE at Home COMPROMISE

REGINALD L. HUDSON

All characters and locations appearing in this work are fictitious. Any resemblance to real persons, living or deceased is purely coincidental.

Copyright © 2009 by Reginald L. Hudson. All rights reserved.

Printed in the United States of America

Publishing services by Selah Publishing Group, LLC, Tennessee. The views expressed or implied in this work do not necessarily reflect those of Selah Publishing Group.

No part of this publication may be reproduced, stored in a retrieval system or transmitted in any way by any means, electronic, mechanical, photocopy, recording or otherwise, without the prior permission of the author except as provided by USA copyright law.

ISBN: 978-1-58930-241-9
Library of Congress Control Number: 2009911956

Cover Designed By Robert Sabol

IN MEMORY

In memory of my father, Deacon Malcolm M. Hudson Sr., who was the epitome of a godly man, husband and father. Because of his inspiration, love and guidance I am becoming the husband, father and Pastor God desires me to be.

I love you and I miss you.

ACKNOWLEDGEMENTS

To my wife and partner Shelly, thank you for your love, wisdom and support. As a team together you allow me to frame the creativity of my ideas as you fill them with balance and perspective. You allow me to be myself and I am a handful, it is a blessing and a joy to begin each day with you by my side. I Laaaa Yooo!

To my best friend, Stephanie Quarles, we have been on a journey together through the highs and lows of life for almost twenty years. Thank you for always believing in me and pushing me to become more, even when I did not want to hear it. When others gathered around for my funeral, you showed up for my resurrection.

To my mother Janice Hudson (a.k.a. Mama Jan) you have been a loving balance in my life and the lives of so many. Thank you for being one of my biggest cheerleaders. I can always count on you to bounce off new ideas and possibilities. It gives me great joy to hear you laugh at my jokes that no one else can appreciate.

ACKNOWLEDGEMENTS

To my mother and father-in-law Nellie (Mama Chick) and Bill (Pop-Pop Bill) thank you for a beautiful daughter (Shelly) to complete my life. Just as important, thank you for opening up your heart and life to me and treating me like a son, rather than an in-law. My heart and love for you cannot be measured in words.

Finally, to my other best friend; because I am blessed to have two, Wayne L. Powell, thank you for the many years of devoted friendship. You too, have been there with me through my wounds and just as important you have been there through my healing. I am so excited at what God is doing in your life, it's because you constantly bless me and others. Let's share the beaches of the world together.

CONTENTS

FOREWORD XIII
INTRODUCTION XV

CHAPTER 1
    A RECIPE FOR A DREAM 17

CHAPTER 2
    ATTITUDE DETERMINES ALTITUDE 21

CHAPTER 3
    CLICK, CLACK, SKIP! 27

CHAPTER 4
    WHAT IF? 35

CHAPTER 5
    TURNING POINTS 47

CHAPTER 6
    SLAYING GOLIATH 57

CHAPTER 7
    JUST GO FOR IT! 65

CONCLUSION 71
ABOUT THE AUTHOR 75

FOREWORD

The hallmark of transformational leadership is the ability to help those you lead envision the possibilities and opportunities that wait before them. While sometimes difficult to explain, such leadership is immediately recognizable to everyone. Transformational leaders inspire personal and corporate change in those who follow them.

Such is the type of leadership of President Getitdone, a fictional character created by Reginald L. Hudson, to lead the failing Muststay College out of its thirty-three year slump. Without vision, the people of Muststay and the surrounding community began to "perish." Little was accomplished and much was lost as Muststay College began a spiral into mediocrity and compromise.

Using a humorous and light-hearted style, *Leave Compromise at Home* explores the impact of hopelessness, lack of vision, and lack of organizational focus on the functioning of an educational institution. However, since the leadership skills that work at Muststay College can easily translate to other types of organizations, this book is appropriate for any group that wants to understand the power of leadership and maximize its own potential.

FOREWORD

Leave Compromise at Home will generate discussions about issues such as how to best achieve organizational goals, how to maintain effective working relationships, how to deal with employees who do not support organizational change, how to celebrate employee success, and how to understand the impact of gender on leadership. The book can be discussed as an entire work. Whatever the method might be, I strongly recommend this book for church groups, educational groups, business groups, and for leaders in any domain. It will certainly generate a great deal of discussion and I believe inspire positive outcomes in the reader.

Tresmaine R. Grimes, PhD
Assistant Vice President for Academic Affairs
Iona College
Associate Pastor, Strait Gate, the Church at Westchester
Founder, Sarah's Daughters Ministries

INTRODUCTION

My only advice to you is read this story and say:

What if?

Enjoy!

Chapter 1

A RECIPE FOR A DREAM

Conveniently tucked away in the heartland of the Midwest located in a small town called Pitiful was Muststay College. In a good year, the enrollment would max out around twenty-seven hundred students on campus. Unfortunately, this college hadn't seen a good year in thirty-three years. They struggled to maintain their Division III NCBB status for their athletic programs. Muststay College hadn't always known lean times. As a matter of fact, when the school was founded in 1936, the town of Pitiful benefited tremendously.

In addition, the morale of the small town of Pitiful was buzzing with excitement as students from Muststay College would invade the small town to relax, shop, and look for a place to have a good time. The town of Pitiful had only forty-nine hundred and three residents. Although small in number, they were very large in hospitality and kindness. It was not uncommon, a few times a week, to find the Muststay students perched around the dinner tables in the modest homes of Pitiful's residents enjoying a home cooked meal. Just about every home had a take out policy that would send students back to their campus with containers filled with a midnight snack. Yeah, Muststay College was in its infancy during those early days under the leadership of a feisty visionary, 30 year old Edwin Clarkston, who was the Founder and President.

President Clarkston, an Easterner, God-fearing and fun-loving man, was known for his stern beliefs when it came to his dreams, morals and values. Whenever President Clarkston would share a plan for the students, faculty, administration, coaches, and employees at Muststay College, he would never have a backup plan. His goal was to work his Plan A until it was successful. His spirit quickly spread like an epidemic and positively affected the students, faculty, administration, coaches, and employees. Even the residents of Pitiful were affected by the positive persona of President Clarkston. He would teach community classes on weekends to the town residents who could not afford to attend the college or whose work schedule did not provide the time. Everyone knew how much President Clarkston loved to teach his favorite subject, *'A Recipe for a Dream.'* He loved the subject so much because his life experience was wrapped up in it. He wanted the residents of Pitiful to know that a dream should not die or be cast aside because of finances, time and most of all past failures. The feisty visionary loved challenging anyone who displayed doubt. His famous quote was known for miles as he would grab you by the arm and pull you nose to nose and say, *"Hey you! Look into my eyes and tell me if you see Compromise."*

For thirty-three years President Clarkston's vision and enthusiasm filled Muststay College and the little town of Pitiful with joy, happiness and prosperity. Every aspect of the college was excelling, even the athletic program. Who would have thought this little college lost in Middle America would achieve national recognition academically with a 93% on-time graduation rate. Muststay's football team the Scrappin Scoundrals were a good team although they never competed for a NCBB Championship. However, each week they were the talk of the town as people would travel for miles from surrounding towns to watch the Scoundrals scrap with their opponents. Their pre-game ritual was always grabbing one another by the face mask and saying, *"Hey you! Look into my eyes and tell me if you see Compromise."* This was certainly a tribute to the impact President Clarkston had on everyone. Their athletic programs; baseball, soccer, field hockey and of course football, became a classroom of discipline, instruction and perseverance on playing fields of sparse blades of grass.

Late in 1977, President Clarkston announced his retirement and that he would be moving back east to New York. This fifty-nine year old visionary was tired; his mind still sharp as a razor, but his body was becoming more and more uncooperative because of health challenges. The town of Pitiful had enjoyed much success and prosperity from Muststay College. No one ever thought about who would carry President Clarkston's visionary dream and plan to a higher realm in the future. No one could imagine that the next thirty-three years would find Muststay College dwelling in obscurity. The President's chair at Muststay College would become a revolving door during those thirty-three years, names without personality or a visionary plan. The classrooms and hallways ached with the absence of the visionary dreamer shuffling his feet down the hallway pulling a struggling student aside and saying, "*Hey you! Look into my eyes and tell me if you see Compromise.*" It's not by coincidence the on-time graduation rate fell from 93% over twenty-nine years to 47% over the next thirty-three. The athletic program had fallen into decline as well; the classroom built on dirt and grass was all but in permanent recess. There were three years the football team which joyously entertained the residents of Pitiful, barely had enough players to field a team.

The only national coverage they would receive was being the laughing stock of the nation. They now owned the longest losing streak in the nation and it was an NCBB record, 0-196-33. Thirty-three seasons and the closest thing to a win for the Scrappin Scoundrals would be thirty-three ties. It was clear the superstar of this football team was not the Quarterback, Running Back or Wide Receiver; it was the Field Goal Kicker. The atmosphere was different now; seldom did you find the students of Muststay College around the dinner tables of the residents of Pitiful. The future direction for the college was uncertain and filled with inconsistency, and it seemed every President would share a plan filled with contingency and backup plans. No longer were the faculty, students, administration, coaches, and employees familiar with President Clarkston's meetings where he would share a Plan A without a backup plan. Now for the next thirty-three years the Presidents who conducted these meetings would present their plan and abandon it at the first sign of trouble or uncertainty.

Chapter 2

ATTITUDE DETERMINES ALTITUDE

It was August and once again Muststay College was preparing for a new President. No one knew who the President would be or where they would come from, and the truth be told not too many cared. The light of excitement, enthusiasm and expectation had dimmed greatly in the life of Muststay College and a town known as Pitiful. However, this particular summer had a different twist to it. Even though the college's eighth President had not yet arrived, there were two strange faces seen meandering around the college campus. Early in June, two women arrived at Muststay College and met with the Board of Trustees, faculty, administration, coaches and employees. The names of these two women were Shenell Hope and Cortney Faith. Initially, those in attendance at this called meeting did so with some resentment. After all Ms. Hope and Ms. Faith were intruding on their summer vacation. The two women explained they would be working on

LEAVE COMPROMISE *at Home*

campus throughout the summer making preparations until the new President arrived around the end of August. One of the faculty members interrupted Ms. Hope and said, "Excuse me! I don't mean to be rude, but who are you and what are you doing here?" Cortney Faith quickly replied, "We came at the request of a long time friend Mr. Edwin Clarkston." At that moment, eyes in the room lit up as you heard a unified gasp, the first sign of unity that had been experienced in years.

Cleavon Goody, the Chair and longest tenured member of the Board of Trustees asked, "How is Edwin doing? I miss my old friend" as he reared back in his seat with a smile of remembrance. Shenell Hope replied, "Mr. Clarkston is doing well in New York and enjoying his retirement." A voice from the back of the roomed echoed out, "Is he still feisty?" The room chuckled but Cortney Faith's laugh became unbearable as if she knew something that needed to be shared. Shenell Hope tried to remain professional, but she too had to give into the moment. The voice from the back of the room asked," What's so funny?" Ms. Faith, now doubled over with tears of laughter, tried to share the story without success, so Shenell Hope interjected. "It's funny you should ask about Mr. Clarkston's feistiness. His health has improved and he teaches a couple days a week at a small college in New York City. He doesn't drive anymore so he moves around the city by subway. Apparently, one day while waiting on the subway platform he heard a young man talking to a friend with a dejected look on his face. He overheard the young man in the conversation talking about how his plans had failed and there was no use in pursuing them anymore. What caught Mr. Clarkston's attention was when he heard the young man say he would just settle for returning home and working at his dad's factory.

Hearing those words Mr. Clarkston rushed over to the two young men talking and grabbed the dejected one by his arm while startling the other and as he pulled him nose to nose he said, *"Hey you! Look into my eyes and tell me if you see Compromise?"* Before Mr. Clarkston could encourage the young man, his friend called the police and had Mr. Clarkston arrested figuring he was a nut." The room broke out into laughter again, and you could hear comments like, "That sounds like the President Clarkston we know and love." There were still a few Muststay College faculty and administration who remembered him while others knew of his reputation and legacy. This light hearted moment is just what those in the room needed after so many years of heartache and disappointment. You could feel everyone embracing Shenell Hope and Cortney Faith. The ladies assured everyone that Mr. Clarkston was doing fine and the charges were dropped when he went to court. It turns out the Judge was one of his students many years prior. When he walked into the courtroom the Judge recognized him, he stood up and shouted, *"Hey you! Look into my eyes and tell me if you see Compromise?"* How can you prosecute after that?

The young man after hearing about Mr. Clarkston's reputation dropped the charges and apologized. Since then both have become good friends and the young man stops by Mr. Clarkston's home often to check on and spend time with him. Ms. Faith chimed in with, "Let's get back to the reason Shenell and I are here. This college is near and dear to the heart of Mr. Clarkston. For many years, he has watched in agony the decline of Muststay College. Before coming here, we met with Mr. Clarkston at his home and asked after thirty-three years, why is he looking to address the conditions of the college now?" He leaned back in his favorite recliner with a pleasant smirk and said, You know, I went to my church a few weeks ago, and I looked at my Pastor who was 38 years old when he came to our church. He was energetic and a dreamer. Although sometimes hard to understand with his views and approaches, he would often challenge our Youth and Adults, and required everyone to cut the word 'Can't' out of their vocabulary. Pastor Huddles would remind all of us that with man things can become impossible, but with God all things are possible."

Pastor Huddles had encouraged everyone who had a specific prayer request to attend the Sunday worship celebration. We were having a wonderful time with songs and fellowship; then at the close of Pastor Huddle's sermon he said two things that shook my spirit and made me think of Muststay College. First he shared, "When opportunity and preparedness meet, great things happen." The second thing he shared as he continued to violate the English grammar, "If you do what most people won't do, you will have what most people won't have." I knew then from my retirement chair in New York, I needed to take ownership of Muststay College's situation and future. Pop-Pop Bill the long time Chief of Campus Security echoed, "It figured after all of these years we still need President Clarkston to come to our rescue." Applause and cheers rang out throughout the room. At that moment Jaryd DeGrumpy stood up. He was the Athletic Director for the school during those thirty-three years of decline and all of the coaches and athletic programs were under his watch. You could say he was the proud owner of the football teams 0-296-33 National record.

DeGrumpy who was known for killing any happy moment that could be encountered interjected, "Excuse me ladies! Enough with the shee-shee poo-poo socialization, I have a golf tee time in a half hour, I would appreciate you getting to your point for being here." Ms. Hope replied, "No problem" and instructed Ms. Faith to share the plan for Muststay College's future. Cortney Faith shared that in order for the new President to be effective, it would require advance preparation from everyone. The first thing that must change is the attitude on campus, a mind filled with negativity is like quick drying cement, there is no room to expand, but only to harden. Secondly, beginning with the Board of Trustees down to the campus security, the conversation must be positive and enlightening. You cannot expect positive results for your future when you spend time talking about the past and what hasn't worked. Finally, begin to look, speak, and act like what you expect this college and the town of Pitiful to become. We must become a model to follow. The definition of a model is a small replica of the real thing. "We know our resources are temporarily limited."

Jaryd DeGrumpy voiced, "What do you mean temporarily?" Shenell Hope replied, "Attitude, Mr. DeGrumpy, attitude. It will determine your altitude in life," continued Cortney. "If you believe in what this college and town can be, then why not take ownership and invest in it?" Over the next two months, pull the resources out of your time and your pockets; bring together the little in order to create much. Pull together as faculty, administration, coaches and employees, paint your classrooms, and develop the campus landscape. Visit the town and encourage the residents to enroll their children in Muststay College, have the merchants' partnership and donate to our college. Let the community know Muststay College is back and we have a plan to rise again.

LEAVE COMPROMISE at Home

This day had been long overdue and for the first time in thirty-three long unfulfilled years, hope and optimism filled the room. Yes, Shenell Hope and Cortney Faith two strangers only two hours earlier had created a pep rally usually reserved for the Athletic Department. As everyone left the room smiling and embracing, the motivation in their smiles simply said, "What if?" Only, Jaryd DeGrumpy, mumbling bolted out of the room golf bag in hand as the joy was too much to endure. During the absence of a President, Trustee Cleavon Goody assumed the interim role and he looked forward to turning over the reigns to the new school President. The summer was moving swiftly and now it was late August and everyone was trying to remain committed to carrying out their assignments. However, no one had a clue who the new President would be and that only fueled Jaryd DeGrumpy's sarcasm and negative attitude.

Chapter Three

CLICK, CLACK, SKIP!

A few days before classes were to begin Trustee Goody received a phone call from a gentleman he did not know. The gentleman said his name was Will U. Trustme in charge of the Executive Search Team in New York. He informed Trustee Goody that the new President would arrive on campus the next morning at 9:00 am. He instructed Trustee Goody to have the faculty, administration, coaches, and employees assembled for a meeting. Without giving a name or any background information Mr. Trustme said, "Have a good evening" and hung up.

It was Thursday morning and the conference room had an atmosphere of anxiety, filled with a touch of excitement. Everyone was nervously chattering amongst themselves while incorporating an occasional glance at the clock which read 8:57 a.m. Surely the new President wouldn't be late for

LEAVE COMPROMISE *at Home*

his first day or would he? Suddenly, you heard the sound of the door opening, the rude screech that had been there too long, and there wasn't enough oil in the town of Pitiful to eliminate it. There were still two days before classes and students would avoid these hallways as long as possible. It could only be one person, yet no one dared to peek their head out of the door. You could hear footsteps in the distance as they echoed off the walls. However, these steps had a different sound. This conference room had become the greeting center for the many past Presidents who took over the reigns. Yet, there was something different about the cadence of this walk. Normally you heard a thump, thump, thump or a shuffling of the feet but this was certainly different. The cadence of this walk had a click, clack, skip-click, clack, skip as it became noticeable a heel was dragging. Suddenly, one of the cafeteria workers jumped up and cried out, "It's a woman! The new President is a woman! Listen!" The cadence now louder became more evident, click, clack, skip, and the other women joyously agreed with a smile.

Athletic Director, Jayrd DeGrumpy, and Trustee Cleavon Goody could no longer resist, they poked their heads out of the door and the results spoke for themselves. It was true! For the first time in the history of Muststay College the click, clack, skip was a woman. As she approached with the sun shining through the hallway windows across her path; her face was partially hidden in the silhouette. Her pace was filled with purpose, there was no looking from side to side in these unfamiliar hallways, she knew the room number and the direction she was headed. She stood about 5'6" borrowing four inches from her stiletto heels, her hair cut close and stylishly cropped, and her eyes were framed by a pair of rectangular glasses with the Dolce & Gabbana signature. Her business suit was a fitted Herringbone a rare sight in the town called Pitiful. Her jewelry was modest but complimented her attire. Finally, how could you miss the camel skin briefcase?

Before they could duck back into the room, the new President was upon DeGrumpy and Goody. She smiled and said, "Good morning gentlemen, pardon me," as she entered the conference room. As she passed DeGrumpy and Goody, they noticed her ring finger was absent of a band of commitment. The gentlemen would have no husband to call to rescue them from the confident persona of this new President. As she approached the front of the room, everyone quickly scurried to find their seats; that is everyone besides Jaryd DeGrumpy who was still a victim of an entitlement mentality. Of course, there were a few who had to posture for brownie points as they came to the front and made themselves known. When the brief exchange concluded, she said, "Good morning Ladies and Gentlemen," with a radiant smile and authoritative tone. "My name is Alicia Yvette Getitdone and it is my pleasure to meet all of you today, especially both of you Mr. DeGrumpy and Mr. Goody. Astonished Jaryd DeGrumpy looked at Goody and said, "She already knows our names." At that moment there was a knock on the conference room door and it opened. President Getitdone acknowledged three students pushing in three carts filled with a variety of donuts, pastries, bagels, juices, coffee, tea and water.

Amazement raced around the room, a voice could be heard saying, "When is the last time something like this happened?" Another voice replied, "About thirty-three years ago." President Getitdone told everyone to eat and enjoy, she told the three students she had arranged for a catered breakfast and dinner for any student already on campus since the cafeteria was not yet opened. Titles and position did not get in the way of the assault on the Getitdone goodies. President Getitdone overheard Jaryd DeGrumpy mumble while reaching for a croissant, "She is already spending money the school doesn't have." To which she replied loud enough to address all in the room who might have thought along the same lines, "Don't worry Mr. DeGrumpy, the breakfast is on my dime the school budget is still in the same pitiful shape," as she smiled and walked away.

President Getitdone distributed packets of information to everyone; the mystery was slowly unveiling itself. On top of the packet was her bio. It mentioned nothing about teaching or experience at any level of College or Secondary Schools. Jaryd DeGrumpy held his head as he read on, mean time Trustee Cleavon Goody read and leaned back with a quiet satisfying smile of relief. Alicia Yvette Gettitdone was somebody! Her sister, Shelly Huddles, was the wife of Mr. Edwin Clarkston's Pastor. Both sisters made their money working together in Corporate Business Ratings, Stocks, Bonds and Treasury note investments, and Clean Energy Development for the Fossil Fuel industry. Shelly ran their New York office while Alicia ran their office out of Hollywood, Florida. It was Shelly Huddles who recommended her sister Alicia Yvette to Mr. Clarkston when she heard of his concern for Muststay College's future. One of the employees while reading the bio said, "This explains the unusual shipment that arrived in Pitiful the other day. It was a custom Jaguar with Florida plates; we had no idea who it belonged to." Everyone ate and read with a look of puzzlement that could be seen on faces as groups formed to discuss what was before them. President Getitdone sensing the change in atmosphere shared, "I noticed as some of you read my bio that your faces seem to show some displeasure."

Pop-Pop Bill, the Chief of Campus Security, said "What a grand entrance you have made today, the food, your attire....." Then Jaryd DeGrumpy said, "I guess the Jag is yours too?" She nodded, "Yes, as a matter of fact it is, is it a problem?" "Would you have preferred I showed up in a Taxi wearing a blouse and khakis? Ladies and gentlemen, a healthy education enhances our dreams, goals and standards for success. A good Plan A is a vehicle that will get you on the right road to achieve. Beyond the classroom as educators, and administrators we have a responsibility to provide a model for our students and community to aspire. A model is..." Trustee Goody replied, "A small replica of the real thing." President Getitdone said, "That's right Trustee Goody, that's right."

"If my Jaguar, that I worked hard for and purchased with my own money, offends you that much I will have it shipped back to Florida only after you answer this one question. If I shouldn't be the rightful owner of such a car, then tell me who should be?" Immediately, you could see shame and embarrassment on many of the faces. One of the custodians, James Polite, broke the tension by saying "Madam President, would you like your car washed and waxed?" Laughter filled the room as the meeting resumed. President Getitdone shared the itinerary for the next two days. She concluded the meeting with, "Please feel free to stay and enjoy the refreshments, please take home what you cannot eat. Beginning this afternoon at 3:00 pm until 3:00 pm tomorrow, I will meet with every Trustee, faculty member, administrator, coach and employee for Strama Relief. "Dean Grady replied, "Madam President, what is Strata....?" President Getitdone, asked "You mean Strama?" it's a simple equation, Stress + Drama=Strama. Every corporation, not for profit, civic, private organization or educational system has some form of

'Strama' in its brain trust. We will meet to eliminate as much of it as we can for now. Oh by the way, tomorrow evening I have secured the Grand Ballroom at the Pitifully Made Hotel. We will have a night of fun, eating and dancing so bring your families. I will take about thirty minutes to share the vision plan then we will party and celebrate new beginnings." The room became chaotic with joy, what an unexpected treat, first breakfast and now dinner and a party. Dean Christopher Grady leaned over to Trustee Goody and said, "When was the last time something like this happened?" With tears in his eyes and a quiet smile on his face he replied, "about thirty-three years ago, yeah, about thirty-three years." At that moment, Shenell Hope and Cortney Faith entered the room and were immediately greeted with hellos and warm embraces. Cortney Faith exclaimed with joy, "I guess all of you have met your new President!" The responses were joyful and very positive; it was clear the thirty-three years of drought without a plan for success was on the verge of ending because Muststay College was alive again and very soon so would be the town called Pitiful.

The opportunity and potential were staring Muststay College in the face, all they needed to do was to develop a Plan A and eliminate a Plan B and leave Compromise at home. Hope and Faith were asked, "Are both of you coming to the dinner dance tomorrow evening? Cortney Faith answered, "We would love to attend, but Shenell and I are on our way to the airport. A moment of sadness blanketed the room, clearly although anonymous and unwelcomed a few months ago, now Shenell Hope and Cortney Faith had found a special place in the heart of the Muststay College family. Shenell Hope said, "Unfortunately duty calls and we must be off to our next assignment." As they headed for the door the hugging and well wishes resumed as Trustee Goody said, "Thank you for sending us our new President, I think a business minded woman will add a special touch here at Muststay College." Ms. Hope and Ms. Faith stepped back and glanced at one another as Shenell Hope replied, "We didn't send her." Once again puzzled looks filled the room, Cortney Faith said, "She's right, we had no idea who the new President would be or where they would come from, with that Ms. Hope and Ms. Faith grabbed their briefcases blew a kiss and waved as they exited the conference room.

Chapter Four

WHAT IF?

The next day, the town called Pitiful was buzzing with excitement, enthusiasm and expectation. Alicia Yvette Getitdone had injected life and hope back into this small once close knit community. The barber shops, hair salons, and clothing stores were filled with patrons and the store merchants had an unusually busy, yet satisfying day as the bell on their cash register rang often. It was clear everyone wanted to look their best for this evenings dinner dance. The thoughtfulness of the town carried over to the car wash as it was reported that a couple of employees of Muststay College wanted to surprise President Getitdone with a wash and wax of her Jag. Rumors have it Jaryd DeGrumpy sprung for the air freshener but that was yet to be confirmed. Although everyone was cautiously optimistic and had not fully embraced President Getitdone and her ideas, she had them thinking,

"What if?" No one could question that in less than 48 hours President Getitdone had changed the atmosphere for Muststay College that had been stale for thirty-three years.

It was amazing how one focused individual with a deep-seeded conviction of what could be, affected a college and a town. Call it coincidence or divine intervention, but the sun seemed to be shining brightly over Pitiful this day. In reality, the sun was shining just as brightly as any day, the difference was today the cloudy outlook for the Muststay College family and the residents of Pitiful was lifting. As expected, the evening was one for the history books for the town called Pitiful. They had had celebrations before, but this was a gala event never before seen. The town of Pitiful was used to celebrations for things that had happened. Tonight Muststay College was celebrating what was about to begin. Upon entering the hotel lobby the faculty, administration, coaches and employees mouths nearly dropped to the floor.

The walls were filled on the left side with historical pictures of some of the most memorable events that had occurred at Muststay College. However, if the left side would cause their mouth to drop what was on the right side of the wall would knock their socks off. Everyone's picture with a brief bio was posted! Now this was truly different. At the registration table next to each name tag was a beautifully decorated glass with a picture of Muststay College and an inscription that read, '*Leave Compromise at Home.*' You would have thought the cocktail hour was the main course with thirty-three varieties of food to snack on. Yeah, thirty-three, as much as this night would celebrate the future, it would certainly say goodbye to the past. Already a few of the Muststay faithful could not resist and were sharing a few of their best dance moves before dinner. It was clear some of them should have eaten first.

No expense was spared on the part of President Getitdone for the Muststay College family; finally as everyone entered the Grand Ballroom, they were dressed in black tie and long evening gowns. The women flaunted the best costume jewelry Pitiful had to offer. As everyone took their seats the level of the celebration was about to rise again, as the waiters, two assigned to each table shared a choice of five entrees. This was totally unheard of but quickly embraced. This was a far cry from any food served previously at the Pitifully Made Hotel. In the midst of the entrée selections someone noticed this was not the normal hotel staff. Their attire with their white serving jackets, jet black pants and razor sharp crease symbolized a level of five star excellence. By the door stood a very tall silver haired man dressed in the uniform colors of the staff but his attire was a Tux; the Pitifully Made Hotel never had a Maitre d' before!

With a String Quartet playing soft music in the background, the mood was festive and everyone was having a good time. Everyone, that is except the Athletic Director Jaryd DeGrumpy. Perched at his table next to Trustee Goody, he could be heard mumbling, "A cocktail hour with thirty-three different foods, most I never heard of, fancy waiters, special glasses and now five entrees and a band!" As the Maitre d' approached the table DeGrumpy said, "Excuse me sir! Who are you and all of these new faces? What happened to the old staff? Some of them were my friends." The Maitre d' replied, "President Getitdone made all of the arrangements. By the way you must be Mr. Jaryd DeGrumpy." To his surprise he nodded his head and said, "How did you know?"

LEAVE COMPROMISE *at* Home

Handing him an envelope he shared, "President Getitdone said I would know you when I saw you." Trustee Goody's quiet demeanor could not hold back the burst of laughter that caused those at his table to join in. As the Maitre d' continued his rounds, DeGrumpy with the usual look of embarrassment opened the envelope while still mumbling, "I wonder how much this dinner dance will cost the college?"

Dear Mr. DeGrumpy,

By now you have met the Maitre d' Juan, and you have seen the gala in the evenings festivities, which I'm sure has raised many questions in your mind. I'm sure your first question was, "I wonder how much this dinner dance will cost the college?" Please do not worry Sir! This dinner dance is on my dime. Oh, by the way, don't worry about the Pitifully Made Hotel staff, they have been given a paid night off with a small stipend to replace the tip they would have received. In addition, dinner arrangements have been made at a restaurant so they can take their families out. Part of building and pursuing a dream is every now and then experiencing what you haven't had so when you receive it, it will not overwhelm you. Then it can become a part of your lifestyle.

Enjoy your evening Mr. DeGrumpy and please have some fun.

Alicia Yvette Getitdone

Everyone was having such a great time that they failed to notice President Getitdone had not yet arrived. Suddenly there was commotion in the back of the room as applause broke out followed by comments of, "Good evening Madam

President." "Wow! You look lovely this evening." As she entered her appearance very different from the professional look she adorned, no business suit, designer glasses or modest jewelry. Tonight she would own the look of elegance as she sashayed through the room smiling and greeting everyone as if they were personal friends. Her only escorts were grace and glamour. Her long black evening wear had a signature of Armani as her diamond necklace and earrings worked in concert trading sparkles. She was still borrowing four inches from her heels which turned the day shift of Ostrich over to the evening shift of Lambskin. It was clear this President wasn't only classy and intelligent but beautiful too. One of the Trustees seated at the dais leaned back taking in the events unfolding before him and reflecting on the past couple of days, he thought, "What if?" He observed the administration, faculty, coaches and employees of Muststay College along with their families exhibiting a joy and enthusiasm that had not been present for thirty-three years. During the dessert hour which consisted of thirty-three varieties, President Getitdone approached the podium. As if cued, everyone stood with cheers and applause as it was clear the events of the evening were greatly appreciated. Everyone in the room felt special and that had been absent for a long time; overwhelmed, President Getitdone had to step back from the podium and even her professional posture could not stop the tear residing in the corner of her eye. This moment had to be real because in the midst of this feast the sight of alcohol was absent to ensure this would be a true family, friend and fellowship gathering.

Athletic Director, Jaryd DeGrumpy, in the midst of the cheers and applause muttered, "This is a cute moment for someone who just arrived and hasn't done anything yet. Enjoy tonight Ms. Getitdone, because tomorrow you must face the real serious issues concerning this college." Once she composed herself President Getitdone stepped back to the podium and began to speak. "First of all, I want to thank all of you for your warm embrace. Honestly, when I arrived a couple of days ago I did not know what to expect other than what I was told. I understand it will take some of you time to embrace me and there is a possibility a few will not. All I can say is regardless of whether we agree or not, or become friends or remain casual acquaintances, there is never a reason not to show one another respect."

"I said I would share Plan A with you this evening and it would be void of a backup plan. I know logic dictates that sound strategy calls for a Plan B in case Plan A does not work. The first thing we must do among our faculty, administration, students, coaches and employees is not to prepare for failure with a backup plan. Beginning tonight after we dance and celebrate, we will leave this place with only a Plan A for the future of Muststay College. No one ever said we would not have to modify, add or subtract from our Plan A, but we will not abandon it. We will approach it with determination, perseverance and conviction. I am asking everyone at Muststay College regardless of your years of service and area of responsibility to take ownership of this Plan A. Study it until you understand it, then once you understand it-teach it to someone else until they can teach it to another. We will know we have a Plan A once we no longer have to think about it, but instinctively live it out daily." Jaryd DeGrumpy began to raise his hand to interject but President Getitdone shaking her head from side to side stopped him, "Not now Mr. DeGrumpy, I promised yesterday a thirty minute vision for the college so this is my time." DeGrumpy slowly slithered back into his chair again wearing the tailor made face of embarrassment.

"We must change the face of our college. We were once high spirited and full of enthusiasm and we will recapture that this fall. I know it's easy to look at what's broken, but it is just as easy to look at what works." A few responses of affirmation could be heard throughout the room. "The thirty-three year past of Muststay College has also had an impact on this town called Pitiful, so tonight our past will become our rearview mirror. We will glance at it from time to time only to remember what we do not want to become and learn from past mistakes. Our front windshield will be our dreams, goals and objectives which consist of our Plan A. Dreams always include people and tonight has been set aside to remind everyone in the Muststay College family you are the dream and it will take all who believe it to make it happen." The room erupted, some began to stand while others high fived and slapped one another on the back. It could be seen at each table that this was more than a vision for a college, this was life being breathed back into a town while recapturing their purpose. Hope and Faith had boarded a plane and departed but excitement, enthusiasm and expectation had become the new residents.

President Getitdone feeling the accomplishment of her vision said, "Finally, after analyzing the thirty-three years of Muststay College, I want you to know that it was not failure that caused this institution to lose hope and slide back into obscurity, no, no it was Compromise and tonight with the power invested in me as your new President, I challenge everyone present to leave Compromise at home." By now the dinner dance had turned into a full blown pep rally as people began moving around the room encountering one another and repeating, "*Leave Compromise at Home.*" "In order to develop a dream you must put 'value' on it and 'sacrifice' behind it. Therefore, I value all who work at Muststay

College, those who will make the dream happen. I know our school budget is on life support, but I will increase everyone's salary by 5% immediately because I am investing in what we shall be. I need all of us to take on a new name called 'Sacrifice.' Our dream and Plan A does not know 9 to 5 but understands some days we must stay until the job is done. That being said, what is our name?" The unified reply was 'Sacrifice' as the jubilation rose even higher at the thought of a raise.

Dean Reginald Meacham had to interject, "President Getitdone what can I say, it seems every time you overwhelm us, you share something else to take us higher. The money you have spent out of your pocket over the past two days, and now a raise." President Getitdone interrupted, "Not so fast Mr. Meacham, these raises will come out of the school budget." Who would have thought the atmosphere could deflate so quickly, even the soft music from the String Quartet stopped playing, the band couldn't play on. One minute pure jubilation the next ultimate disappointment and humiliation as the room filled with a deafening silence. All but Jaryd DeGrumpy who could be heard laughing with sarcasm as he said, "Now I think I'll have a piece of that thirty-three year old dessert." Dean Meacham still in shock clearing his throat, "We barely make payroll now." Glaring at Reginald Meacham, President Getitdone replied, "We will do it with renewed thinking. My sister shares what my brother-in-law Pastor Huddles, teaches all the time and it's two simple principles: 1) "If you do what most people won't do, you'll have what most people won't have." 2) "In life people do what they want to do, if they want to do it bad enough."

"Reginald Meacham, if you and all those gathered in this room believe what I have shared tonight and dare to put aside the obstacles and say, What if? We will achieve our goal. Let's not forget our new name, what is it?" With heads hung the room reluctantly replied, "Sacrifice." A faculty member inquired, "President Getitdone, where do we begin?" President Getitdone replied, "By learning how to fish again, as opposed to waiting for someone to give us one." Dean Meacham with a puzzled look responded, "What do you mean?"

At that moment the new Dean of Admissions, Alexis Enrollemin, said, "Our Athletic program! Our football team the Scrappin Scoundrals use to be our college cash cow and the town of Pitiful benefited too." Pop-Pop Bill chimed in, "You're right, if we could get our football team back on track we could generate enough revenue to get us back on our feet." To which Athletic Director DeGrumpy mumbled, "Try winning anything with that bunch, our greatest victory over the last thirty-three years has been a tie."

Dean Alexis replied, "I'm fairly new here, but I have read the history and this town called Pitiful would literally close down for three hours on a Saturday afternoon to watch the Scrappin Scoundrals, not to mention those who travelled from other neighboring towns. People! What if?" DeGrumpy, now fully irritated that hope would inspire, said, "Do you know how many years ago that was?" A unified response with anger towards DeGrumpy said, "Yes, about thirty-three years ago." DeGrumpy replied, "You expect this football team 0-296-33, to be the answer to your Plan A? Getitdone replied, "Grumpy, YES I DO!" It was evident Muststay College was about to see a side of President Getitdone they didn't ask for. She recomposed herself and apologized to Mr.

LEAVE COMPROMISE at Home

DeGrumpy and those in the room, "Forgive me, I shouldn't have lost my composure." "I agree with Dean Alexis Enrollemin, our football team is the answer to our Plan A; however we are going to have to change our approach in order to live up to our name the Scrappin Scoundrals." At that moment, President Getitdone looked towards the back of the room and signaled a gentleman to come forward. "I would like to introduce one of my immediate changes as we begin our Plan A tonight. Please help me welcome our new head football coach Mr. Joaquin Turnitaround." With star struck eyes and whispers filled with confusion there was scattered applause. Coach Joaquin Turnitaround walked towards the podium with a quick pace, as if he had some place to go. His posture oozed confidence and purpose that commanded respect. President Getitdone shared Coach Turnitaround's bio and resume which read like a Who's Who. He was an academic All-American and very accomplished in the Arts. To his credit, he had written a few plays and musical productions, one that was being cast off Broadway in New York. In addition he was a master choreographer, and he used his playwrighting and dance skills to increase the confidence and abilities in those he trained. There was only one problem and it was major; Joaquin Turnitaround had no football experience.

President Getitdone turned the podium over to Coach Turnitaround and by now the former Head Coach Doubtannini had found a seat next to DeGrumpy as both sat with scowls on their faces and arms folded. Coach Turnitaround spoke, "Good evening, I know this evening has been full of the unexpected, but if you would give me a couple of minutes I would like to share the role I will play in the Plan A President Getitdone has presented." It took a few moments but Coach Turnitaround spoke with so much passion and certainty that even the resistors of change had to once again loosen up and were saying to themselves, "What if?" Coach Turnitaround spoke of capturing the intangibles it takes to be a success, not only on the football field but also in life. He shared he wanted to prepare these young men who play the game every Saturday for the game of life you play everyday. The only difference, in football when challenged you can call timeout, in life you must work through your challenges while the clock continues to run.

Athletic Director DeGrumpy could not resist taking a degrading shot at the new Head Coach, "Excuse me Sir! Who are you and where did you come from since I did not hire you. That withstanding, how can you coach a Division III NCBB football team and you have never coached even a Little League Team?" Turnitaround responded, "Mr. De-Grumpy you are 100% right, I am not a football coach, but more importantly I am a Destiny Coach. The rules will be different and some of the techniques I will use will be unorthodox, but if the coaching staff and team will trust me it will work. Finally, and especially to you Mr. DeGrumpy, in a football game if you fumble you may lose the game, in life if you fumble you can lose your job, family or even your life." There was dead silence in the room and Jaryd De-Grumpy could only slide down in his chair again, adjust his tie and sip his Ginger Ale on the rocks. Coach Turnitaround seized the moment of silence to introduce his coaching staff. "I would like to present the coaches that will work with me. By the way, the current coaches will retain their positions. Only Coach Doubtannini will be reassigned within our Athletic Department. Coach Heartiman will be our Issues Coach dealing with the off field situations our players face. Coach Souliman will be our Spiritual Development Coach helping our players shape their morals, ethics and values; Coach

LEAVE COMPROMISE *at Home*

Wordly is our Conversation Coach. He will help our players learn to speak and converse correctly. Finally, Coach Mindly will be our Thoughts Coach. If there aren't any more questions, I feel the dance floor calling me." Chuckles began to ring out as the expressions on the faces said, this is different but, "What if?"

As Coach Turnitaround departed from the podium a voice rang out, "Coach! the closest we have come to a win is thirty-three ties." Coach Turnitaround replied, "It's sad when your Field Goal Kicker is the superstar of your team..." De-Grumpy interrupted, "He kept us from losing thirty-three more games, and I tell my coaches every game day, 'Let's look good out there.' Turnitaround with a look of annoyance rebuttled, "How good can you look in defeat or even a tie?" President Getitdone returned to the podium to wrap things up before the dancing would begin, "There it is the dream, direction, and Plan A for Muststay College." Trustee Cleavon Goody looked intently into the eyes of President Getitdone and asked, "Do you really believe this Plan A as you call it will work?" She came down from the podium and leaned over the table face to face and said, *"Hey you! Look into my eyes and tell if you see Compromise."*

Chapter Five

TURNING POINTS

A voice cried out, "You know him? He sent you didn't he? Where did you meet him?" President Getitdone once again had the attention of the room, even Jaryd DeGrumpy wanted to know. With laughter in her voice and a sigh of relief that the final piece of the mystery was being unveiled. Getitdone, said, "It's time to dance and celebrate," as she cued the band and began a little salsa step sharing her Latina roots. Professor Diggs interrupted the mood, "We can dance in a minute but how did you meet President Clarkston?" Bringing her salsa slide step to an abrupt halt President Getitdone said, "You already know my sister Shelly initially recommended my name to Mr. Clarkston, but it wasn't until I visited my family in New York last Christmas that I actually met him. I was looking forward to the break and having fun with my family and old friends that I went to school with; the last thing on my mind was work or any discussion of it."

LEAVE COMPROMISE *at Home*

Gazing upward, as if to recall the events in detail, "The Sunday before Christmas there was a special service and my crazy brother-in-law preached his Christmas sermon in a Santa Claus suit for all the children! We had a great time. Anyway, after the service we were all going out to dinner and as we passed the fellowship hall there was this distinguished, elderly gentleman sitting with his cane dining on a bagel. As I turned and looked at him he smiled and winked and said, "Hello Darling!" Before I could respond my sister, Shelly, said, "Hi Mr. Clarkston, this is my sister Alicia, the one I spoke to you about regarding the school." To which I replied to Shelly, "What school, giiiiirrrrrrl, what are you up to?" Mr. Clarkston smiled and Shelly giggled, meanwhile Santa Claus was saying let's go because he's hungry although no longer in his attire. To make a long story short, we invited Mr. Clarkston to dinner with us and that is where he shared his life story and his love for Muststay College. His conversation oozed with wisdom, passion and conviction; however, this distinguished gentleman began to cry as he spoke about what Muststay College used to be. He shared how a once vibrant school had lost its plan for direction and had slipped deeply into the recession of mediocrity and compromise. I inquired, "What would it take for this college to recover?"

My sister responded, "Someone like you!" Mr. Clarkston nodded in agreement and said, "Shelly told me all about you and you have the qualifications, but more importantly the heart and compassion it takes for Muststay College to move forward." Obviously, the rest is history because I'm here. Now, can we dance?" Once again she began her salsa steps and said, "Okay, everyone grab your partner." Professor Bunch said, as everyone was pairing off, "I'm sorry you didn't have an escort for the dinner dance tonight. She replied, "Who said I didn't." At that moment a voice from the back of the room shouted, *"Hey you! Look into my eyes and tell me if you see Compromise."* Could Muststay College stand anymore surprises? Sure enough dressed up in a black Tuxedo with a white vest, shirt, bow tie, and spit shine shoes, it was none other than former President Clarkston. When they realized who it was they began to rush toward President Clarkston and mobbed him with hugs and tears from both the men and the women. Not only had the sun shined brightly in the town called Pitiful but the moon was clearer than it had been for years, let's say about thirty-three years.

Over the next three months, President Getitdone and her Plan A for Muststay College was in full affect. Like any plan in life there are those who immediately jump on board while others examine and scrutinize as they participate at a slower pace. Of course, there are those who will sit back in the cut as resistors of change, especially if their name and abilities are not at the forefront of the dream. Even when their Plan A ran into obstacles, a few would justify abandoning the Plan A and taking another course. President Alicia Yvette Getitdone would rally the faculty, administration, coaches and employees together in the conference room where their journey began months ago. The meeting would last all of five minutes as she would encourage them by saying, "Keep on planning to work, and continue to work our plan." As she would always close her meetings she would encourage the room by saying, *"Hey you! Look into my eyes and tell me if you see Compromise?"*

Of course, during this time period Athletic Director, Jaryd DeGrumpy, would stay far enough away not to enhance the dream and Plan A but close enough to be a hindering presence. It is true you; really do not have a quality dream until someone tries to steal, hinder, or kill it. It's at that moment you must determine whether it's worth fighting for. The change began ironically not on the Muststay College campus but in the town of Pitiful. Suddenly, the dormant weekends were beginning to buzz again as the town merchants revived their stores and Mom and Pop eateries renovated and painted. A few even went as far as to change their menus. One thing about a Plan A, if you stick with it and keep working it daily you do not know when or where the 'pop' will happen. It was happening in the town called Pitiful as the college students once again could be found around the dinner tables of the local residents and of course, they would leave with take out packages.

As for the Scrappin Scoundrals football team, Coach Turnitaround's contribution to the Plan A was taking shape in every category except the win column. The football team had been more competitive than they had been in many years. The Assistant Coaches were doing a great job of preparing their hearts with enthusiasm, their minds with the right attitude and their words now filled with encouragement and conviction. However, with all of this it did not translate to victories on the football field. They were 0-5-2, yes two more ties that could have been wins but as the games were winding down and they had a chance to go for the win, Athletic Director DeGrumpy, as he had for many years, would scream through the headsets of the coaches, "Don't take a chance, kick the field goal at least we will get a tie." Even with the new coaching staff they had to listen to their boss. Sometimes in life there are people who do not play to win, instead they play not to lose.

Out of frustration Coach Joaquin Turnitaround requested a meeting with President Getitdone. He could not bear coming so close to victory and continuously being overruled by Athletic Director DeGrumpy. Coach Turnitaround, said, "Madam President, the Plan A is working and can work even greater if we stop going for the tie. There are times we should have gone on fourth down for the win. Instead I look up and our Field Goal Kicker, Emanuel Compromise, is trotting onto the field in pursuit of another tie." By now, Jaryd DeGrumpy was gaining allegiance from his former Head Coach Seymour Doubtannini and some of the assistant coaches who wanted to go back to the old regime. A follow-up meeting this time called by President Getitdone had the former President Edwin Clarkston, her sister and brother-in-law Shelly and Pastor Huddles, Jaryd DeGrumpy and Coach Joaquin Turnitaround present. It was clear this would be a take no prisoners meeting, Alicia Yvette Getitdone had called in the troops from whom she drew her inspiration and encouragement. She learned a long time ago you must have balance in your dream and your Plan A. On your left needs to be those you empower and inspire and on your right you need those who empower and inspire you. Today, she was leaning to the right by having her sister, brother-in-law and President Clarkston in the meeting. President Getitdone shared, "It has become all too apparent there are obstacles in our Plan A as it pertains to our football team. Coach Turnitaround has implemented ideas and techniques that are bearing positive fruit but it seems Mr. DeGrumpy you and your negative thinking have become a bad seed."

DeGrumpy pounding his fist on the table said, "I've sat back and endured these changes long enough, all I hear everyday all day long, work your Plan A, Hey you! Look into my eyes....ahhh! We need a backup plan and we need it now, we are no better off now than we were when you arrived, and who are these people?" Sarcastically, pointing his finger at Shelly and Pastor Huddles. President Getitdone said, "Someone who can help you leave your Compromise at home. There will be no more talk of a Plan B, C, D, E, or F, do I make myself clear Mr. DeGrumpy?" She removed her glasses so the anger of her eyes could penetrate the stubbornness of his soul. Still borrowing four inches from her custom made shoes, at that moment Alicia Yvette Getitdone stood six feet tall. All Jaryd DeGrumpy could do was return the piercing stare as the warfare over the dream and Plan A was in full effect.

DeGrumpy began to respond but President Clarkston interrupted him, "Jaryd! Listen to the lady she knows what she is doing." Visibly upset Shelly Huddles broke the clasp of her husband's hand that had occurred not out of romance, but more out of prayer. She moved beside her sister and put her arm around her. No one had seen this side of President Getitdone before, with tears in her eyes. Yes, a dream filled with purpose and passion comes with some breaking points and if your dream is not worth crying over it wasn't much of a dream to begin with. Getitdone lifted her head while wiping her tears and with a broken voice addressed Coach Turnitaround, "Joaquin, do you feel our Plan A still has possibilities?" The optimism in Coach Turnitaround surfaced as he said, "Not only does it have possibilities but it has already produced results." He looked sternly at DeGrumpy and said, "My coaching staff has done a superb job in impacting the lives of the Scrappin Scoundrals with the intangibles that are producing results in the classroom first." President Getitdone smiled slightly still while wiping tears from her face as Turnitaround continued, "Seventeen Scrappin Scoundrals have had their names removed from the academic probation list, eight others have qualified for the Dean's List, and Dean Reginald Meacham informed me this morning, are you ready for this?" De-Grumpy throws his head slightly back in a circular motion suffering from the distress of possible good news. Shelly Huddles all smiles says, "Yeah! Bring it." Coach Turnitaround said, as he became a little choked up, "Out of eleven seniors on our team, eleven are now on target for graduation, three in January and the remaining eight in May."

Edwin Clarkston could not help to inquire about more proof the Plan A was working, "Turnitaround, is there anything else?" Coach Turnitaround replied, "Yes, there is Mr. Clarkston, last year four players were arrested for disorderly conduct and now they have received certificates for their community service, but they continued their contributions after they had served their time. Two other players had serious family issues and received very little, if any correspondence, from their families. Since we implemented our Plan A they have reached out to their families and practiced the principles we taught them. Their families came to Pitiful and saw them play for the first time in four years. Unfortunately, the game ended in a tie." Coach Turnitaround looked at Jaryd DeGrumpy as the culprit.

President Clarkston struggled to get to his feet which meant only one thing; they were in for a profound moment. "Jaryd, you are all for getting rid of this Plan A aren't you?" DeGrumpy replied, "Absolutely because this plan does not allow us to build on our strengths," President Clarkston replied, "I beg to differ my old friend. You don't rebuild on your strengths, you rebuild through your weaknesses so they too can become your strengths and not derail your plan. Coach Turnitaround, the two games you tied this year do you really think you could have won them?" Coach Turnitaround nodded with affirmation then said, "President Clarkston, sir, before every game Athletic Director DeGrumpy would come into the locker room and give that same thirty-three year old speech, "Hey! Make us look good out there today even if you don't win." If that isn't Compromise then I don't know what is. Both ties we were facing fourth down inside our opponents ten yard line. Our last tie the ball was on the two yard line with about twenty-four seconds left."

DeGrumpy barked out, "Yeah! Twenty-four seconds left, no timeouts and it was fourth down. If we didn't make it we would surely loose." Coach Turnitaround stood and threw his whistle on the floor, "Mr. DeGrumpy, you are the school's Athletic Director and my boss and at the risk of sounding disrespectful I apologize in advance, but sometimes you must go for what you believe at the risk of taking a loss." "The last game with it all on the line I looked up from my clipboard only to hear Mr. DeGrumpy's voice in my ear saying don't take a chance, go for the sure thing, let Emanuel Compromise kick the field goal." Jaryd DeGrumpy said, "I did what was best for our team and the school!" President Getitdone interrupted, Coach who do we play this week? Turnitaround replied, "This is a tough road game, we play our rivals Datson College and to boot it's their Homecoming game.

President Getitdone surveying the room by now exhausted from intense debate, she noticed her brother-in-law had been silent and expressionless throughout this discussion. "Pastor Huddles, can you add anything to this discussion before we leave?" Pastor Huddles stood and after putting on his overcoat and Kangol hat assisted his wife with hers. He looked back at the room as he reached for the door and said, "If you do what most people won't do, you'll have what most people won't have," and the Huddles departed the room. President Getitdone now back in full posture shared with those who remained, "We will continue to pursue and push our Plan A, however there are times in every dream and the plan associated with that dream, you must discover the turning points. In extreme measures, you must even create them. Gentlemen, we are facing extreme measures so this week whatever it takes we will create the necessary turning points to win. Have a good evening." That night while lying in bed restless, tossing and turning Alicia Yvette Getitdone sat up distressed and turned on the light. She was chewing on her own words that turning points in a dream and the plan that accompanies them sometimes must be created. She looked at her precious pooch who faithfully camped out on the foot of the bed nightly and said,"Peanut! This week I will create the turning point!" Peanut looked at her and barked one time, Getitdone took that as confirmation and said, "Peanut, from your bark to God's ears." She turned out the light, rolled over and went to sleep.

Chapter Six

SLAYING GOLIATH

Early Saturday morning President Getitdone made a surprise visit to Coach Turnitaround's office. This was the first time she had visited the Athletic Field House. Some of the players had arrived early to get taped and treated for existing injuries but she could hear the words of confidence echoing out of their mouths, "We're going to get them today! Hey, no compromise today, this is our game." That delighted President Getitdone's ears and spirit as she branded the school colors. She had arranged for seven buses to take the band, cheerleaders and student body to the game. In addition, she arranged for thirty-three vans to bring the residents of Pitiful to the game. Never before, even under President Clarkston's regime had anything like this been done.

LEAVE COMPROMISE at Home

Today, there would be a pep rally on wheels. President Clarkston, Pastor and Shelly Huddles joined President Getitdone at the locker room as they prayed with Coach Turnitaround, his coaches and team. As Pastor Huddles closed his prayer he said, "Today Gentlemen, just simply go out there and 'GET-IT-DONE!" Following the prayer President Getitdone intercepted Athletic Director, Jaryd DeGrumpy, heading towards the team bus. As he tried to go around her, she said, "Good morning Mr. DeGrumpy." DeGrumpy hastily replied, "Good morning Madam President, how are you? Excuse me please." Blocking his path like the Scoundrals best blocking guard she inquired, "where are you going?" Looking frustrated, DeGrumpy said, "I'm headed to the bus Madam President." She quickly grabbed him by the arm, "not today Sir!" DeGrumpy showing resistance said, "What do you mean?" Pastor Huddles opened the rear door to her Jag, as Getitdone replied, "Today, you will ride to the game with us, you will also sit in the booth with the coaches, and we will sit with you. By this time, the Scrappin Scoundrals were making their way to the team bus, President Getitdone stood by the locker room and stopped one of the players as he was coming out. "Excuse me young man." With a perplexed look on his face he said, "Yes, President Getitdone." She replied, "You look like a fast runner and I need a favor, I left an important blue folder in the faculty conference room, on the table, could you get it for me?" The player replied, "But, President Getitdone, the bus is about to leave!" She looked at him and said, "Then I guess you better get moving." He gazed at President Getitdone and took off running. He never paid attention to the fact that the faculty conference room was a quarter mile from the field house and up a long hill.

Sweating profusely he reached the building and proceeded to the conference room. When he opened the door he saw the blue folder on the table but he noticed it had his name on it.

> To: Mr. Emanuel Compromise
> Enjoy!

He opened the folder and the note told him to enjoy the food and other refreshments. At that moment two campus security police stepped in and as he continued reading he realized they would stay with him throughout the afternoon. A radio had been provided so all of them could listen to the game. The door was immediately locked and Emanuel Compromise realized he might as well make the best of an awkward situation.

Meantime back at the Field House, Coach Turnitaround after taking roll call was a little antsy. President Getitdone inquired, "Coach is there a problem, you look a little worried?" Coach Turnitaround responded, "Yes, I do not see our Field Goal Kicker Emanuel Compromise." Getitdone trying to look surprised said, "I sent one of your players to retrieve my folder out of the faculty conference room maybe it was him." As Coach Turnitaround described him, President Getitdone verified it was him and winked. Turnitaround said, "The bus has to leave now!" President Getitdone re-assured Coach Turnitaround that they would bring him to the game, so Coach Turnitaround smiled and boarded the bus and left.

The game was a war in progress and the elements were not cooperating. It was bitterly cold and the ground was muddy. The wind that day wore an overcoat as it blew briskly throughout the stadium. The Scrappin Scoundrals were impressive as they held their own against the 6 and 1 Datson Bobcats. These Scoundrals may have been 0-5-2, but today they were here to play and represent Muststay College and residents of the town called Pitiful. The game was knotted at 0-0 but was filled with action packed excitement. There were great runs from the line of scrimmage, awesome stops on fourth down, not to mention great catches in blistering cold weather but still there was no score. The longer the Scrappin Scoundrals competed the louder the chants came from the students of Muststay College and the residents of the town called Pitiful. "Hey Bobcats, look into our eyes and tell me if you see Compromise?" The chants in the bitter cold rocked the stadium and the enthusiasm of the Datson Bobcats Homecoming was dwindling with anxiety. Normally, colleges select opponents for their Homecoming they know they can beat. This ensures a festive occasion and allows the seniors playing in their last game a good chance of leaving with a win. Not today, apparently someone forgot to send the Scrappin Scoundrals the memo to rollover and play dead.

DeGrumpy pinned in the Coaches booth between President Getitdone and Clarkston was restless as he listened to the Offensive Coordinator for the Scoundrals sending in the plays. These Offense and Defensive Coordinators would always sit up in the booth because they would have a better view of the field and the players. They could see what their opponents were doing and the defense could counter it, while taking advantage of things they could do on offense. These coordinators seemed to thoroughly enjoy doing their job that day without the intrusion of Athletic Director Jaryd DeGrumpy, for all intents and purposes he was under house arrest. Halftime came and the chants from the Scrappin Scoundrals faithful became more intense, "Hey you Bobcats! Look into our eyes and tell me if you see Compromise?" All

President Clarkston could do was sit back and smile while the mustard from his hot dog froze in the corner of his mustache. What a tribute to a legendary motivator. As the third quarter began the issue was still very much in doubt. Coach Turnitaround was pleased with the intensity of his teams play. It seemed with each down and possession the Scoundrals were gaining confidence. The defense looked like the Berlin Wall as the Bobcats were unable to penetrate. They made the Bobcats running backs regret playing their position. On offense, the Scoundrals were running the ball effectively through the cold, damp, muddy field but just could not get close enough to score.

Coach Turnitaround as he paced the sidelines could be heard saying under his breath as he looked at his clipboard, "What if?" Like a virus, the other coaches throughout the third quarter and into the fourth began to tell the players, "What if?" Yes, as the final quarter began, the Scrappin Scoundrals who were used to past Homecoming games with the Datson Bobcats; where by now it would be a blow out, didn't find that today. President Getitdone looked at her sister in the booth as they clasped hands in a sisterly moment, no words were spoken but Shelly's look at Alicia said, "Sis, I'm proud of what you have accomplished." Alicia's look at Shelly said, "Thanks for believing in me." There was no room for jealousy or envy among these sisters. Their mother, Nellie, (a.k.a. Mama Chick) had raised them right.

The elements by now were not cooperating; if anything they were becoming worse, as a borderline sleet-drizzle was making the playing field unbearable. The thought was beginning to circulate through the minds of many. "Would anybody score today?" Needless to say Jaryd DeGrumpy was beside himself and becoming very verbal, "I need to go down

LEAVE COMPROMISE at Home

onto the field, I always do! Let me out of this booth!" Of course President Getitdone in her wisdom had two Security Guards posted at the door of the coaches' booth. Wherever DeGrumpy would go they would escort him and promptly return him back to the booth. Considering the coaches booth had all of the amenities and facilities there was nowhere to go. With everyone standing and hanging on every play the clock now became the enemy of both teams as it showed 3:42 remaining. The players on both teams were tired and had given everything they could. Certainly, when you are pursuing a dream you must leave all of your heart, soul and effort on the field. This way, if you should fall short, you do not have to live with Old Man Regret and wonder what you could have done differently. However, it was apparent today the Scrappin Scoundrals did not come to look good, they came to slay Goliath.

Just when things seemed to favor the Scoundrals a setback occurred on their own 38 yard line. It was fourth down and they needed to punt. Their punter Joshua Surefoot took the snap and when he went to punt the ball his back foot slipped out from under him in the mud. The ball never touched his foot and the scramble was on as players from both the Bobcats and Scoundrals leap frogged across one another in the icy slush trying to recover the ball. By the time the Bobcats recovered it, the ball was even closer to the Scoundrals goal line as it rested on the 26 yard line. The Bobcat fans were in a frenzy, now they had a chance to chant back to the Scoundrals and their fans that humiliating chant, "Oooops there it is!" Getitdone, Clark, the Huddles and the coaches in the booth were stunned. Only DeGrumpy seemed to have a sigh of relief as he said, "Well, at least we looked good out there today. Could I have another hot dog please?"

Tick, tock, tick, tock 2:55 remaining as the Bobcats lined up their offense and began to move the football with renewed determination, no longer did the Berlin Wall challenge them. They pushed the football over five plays down inside the twelve yard line. On second down, the Bobcats fumbled and the game of leap frog began again but they recovered losing five yards and more importantly precious seconds, tick, tock, tick, tock. Third down and the muddy football once again slipped out of the hands of the Bobcat's Quarterback who quickly fell on it and called timeout with only 1:13 left. What irony as Coach Turnitaround looked across the field to see the Bobcat's Field Goal Kicker trotting out or better yet sliding onto the field. The Scoundrals had two timeouts left but decided to use one just before the Bobcats kicked the field goal. It was a much used strategy to 'Ice the Kicker,' which means give him time to think and hopefully get nervous. This timeout was gutsy because the Scoundrals would not have much time left when they received the ball back. Even with the timeout the effects did not bother the Bobcat's kicker as he put the ball straight through the goal post with room to spare. Maybe the best the Scoundrals could do was look good today in defeat.

Chapter Seven

JUST GO FOR IT!

The teams lined up for the kick off with 56 seconds on the clock. In the coaches booth, President Getitdone could only stare because her thoughts had now left the stadium and were traveling down the highway of reflection. She reflected on the first day as she walked down the halls of Muststay College seeing Jaryd DeGrumpy and Cleavon Goody poking their heads out of the door like two college students looking for mischief. She could not help but to reflect on the night at the dinner dance when she shared the dream and the Plan A for Muststay College and the role the Scrappin Scoundrals would play. She recalled the low points of the dream and the Plan A with doubters sitting in the wings waiting and some even hoping it would fail. She also remembered the meeting with her sister, brother-in-law, Coach Turnitaround, President Clarkston and DeGrumpy, where she had to tell them sometimes you must create the turning points. Now

LEAVE COMPROMISE at Home

she was standing in the midst of the most action packed high intensity game that the Scrappin Scoundrals had played in thirty-three years.

Now the game had become a chess match between the two Head Coaches. You would think the Bobcats would kick the ball as long and as far as possible but they wanted the element of surprise. They kicked a short onside kick hoping as both teams would scramble for it the clock would run down and maybe the Bobcats would recover ending the game. The ball was kicked and skidded across the 50 yard line as the game of leap frog began for the third time. However, the Scoundrals quickly recovered the ball but the time on the clock was uncooperative, 38 seconds and only one timeout. DeGrumpy trying to yell over the voices of the coaches in the booth, "Try to get into field goal range and go for the tie," an all too familiar sound and one that had frankly grown old. As the Scoundrals came to the line of scrimmage, the roar of the crowd was deafening and it was hard for the players to hear the Quarterback signals. Somehow the snap of the ball came on-time as he dropped back to throw only the fifth pass of the day, but the elements were too rude and even the flight of a football was unwelcomed today. The ball sailed down the middle of the field into the arms of a Scrappin Scoundral receiver who caught it at the 31 yard line and dragged two Bobcat defenders six more yards down to the 25 yard line as they quickly lined up to run another play 26 seconds, tick, tock, tick, tock. The ball was snapped and with the same receiver open in the end zone the wind caught the pass as it sailed and it hit the goal post and bounced away.

The clock did not lie; 13 seconds stood between defeat or What if? Coach Turnitaround called the final time out and put on the Coaches headset to talk to the Coaches in the booth. DeGrumpy operating at maximized rudeness was screaming with insanity, "For God sake, kick the field goal." Getitdone suddenly had a look of intense discomfort, she remembered she had sent one of the players on a bogus errand and failed to bring him to the game. The Coaches in the booth echoed the words Coach Turnitaround did not want to hear, "Coach, we have no choice send in Emanuel Compromise to kick the field goal, at least we'll get out of here with a tie." Thoroughly annoyed Coach Turnitaround screamed for Emanuel Compromise but there was no response, others screamed for him too and still no response. Then Coach Turnitaround remembered the wink President Getitdone gave him back at his office when he was taking roll call and Emanuel Compromise was absent.

With a sense of joy and relief Turnitaround told the Coaches in the booth Emanuel Compromise is nowhere to be found. The Offensive Coordinator inquired, "Well, where is he?" To which President Getitdone stepped forward tapping the Coach to get his attention, "We left Compromise at home." With a satisfying smirk she said, "So coach you need to work your Plan A and I advise you to work it quickly." "Sometimes you have to create your own turning points, now is the time." With anxiety all over his face and desperation resting on his shoulders the Offensive Coordinator sarcastically looked at Pastor Huddles and said do you have any suggestions from above?" To which Pastor Huddles replied, "No, but I do have an earthly one, "If you do what most people won't do, you'll have what most people won't have." At that moment it clicked in the Offensive Coordinator's head, "Coach Turnitaround! I got it, run 22 Getitdone right, salsa slide step trap!" Turnitaround said, "Gutsy, but it just might work."

LEAVE COMPROMISE *at Home*

Sitting on the bench was a fifth year senior running back listed at 5'3' and 135 lbs, Coach Turnitaround summoned him to go into the game. This play was developed one day in practice because the players were having fun imitating the two step salsa and slide move President Getitdone did at the dinner dance. This was designed more for training the players to have quick feet and improve their skills but in these bad weather conditions a little razzle, dazzle might make the difference since the Bobcats would be looking for a pass. At 5'3" Christopher Quickfoot could be the difference, if he could just slip past the line of scrimmage. The teams lined up as the stadium rocked to its own beat. Today the Scrappin Scoundrals, Muststay College and the residents of a town called Pitiful would not Compromise, they would GO FOR IT!

The ball was snapped and the entire offensive line stood up and took two steps back and slid to the right with a half wiggle. Astonished, the Bobcats hesitated trying to figure out what was going on, meantime little 5'3" Christopher Quickfoot ran behind the Quarterback who held the ball behind his back and as Christopher Quickfoot took it running around the left side he had a caravan of three blockers in front of him urging him to follow while yelling, "What if Christopher Quickfoot, what if?" The Bobcats suddenly realized they had been out salsa'd and could not recover as little 5'3" Christopher Quickfoot turned the corner heading up the left sideline into the end zone as the clock ran out. Getitdone broke out into the salsa reprisal with her sister Shelly joining her. There is a rumor that Pastor Huddles did his version of the salsa shake but that could not be confirmed. President Clarkston grabbed Getitdone and said, "Darling! Look into my eyes. Today there was no Compromise." The field was saturated by the Muststay and Pitiful faithful fans forgetting the cold weather. For the next two hours they would celebrate on the Datson Bobcats field. Funny isn't it, sometimes you will celebrate your victory and your Plan A in the presence of your enemies. The team hoisted Coach Turnitaround, President Getitdone and President Clarkston on their shoulders and paraded them around the field. As Jaryd DeGrumpy stood shocked on the field and the players paraded President Clarkston past him on their shoulders, President Clarkston leaned down to DeGrumpy and said, "You see what can happen when you leave Compromise at home?"

The Scrappin Scoundrals went on to win their remaining games and ended their season 6-5-2. You would have thought they had won the NCBB National Championship, and in a way they did. They won the Championship of "What if?" The future of Muststay College was bright and the town residents of Pitiful convinced President Getitdone to run for Mayor. She did and won by a landslide. Her first official act as Mayor was to change the name of the town of Pitiful to the town of POTENTIAL! Sometimes you just need to ask yourself, What if?

CONCLUSION

What is Compromise and a Plan A?

I hope you have enjoyed this story and during your reading you have been enlightened and motivated to pursue and/or re-capture your dream. The motivation to write this story occurred out of some personal experiences, but also by encountering many people who are in the *corporate, religious, entertainment, athletic, white collar, blue collar* and *no collar* world. The common thread is, they all had dreams at one point and great desires to achieve them. The difference between accomplishing and still pursuing in many cases involved *Compromise*, a word that is more deadly than failure. I think you know what I mean, those mornings you wake up filled with purpose and excitement, you can see and feel what you want to accomplish. It's already outlined in your head and heart long before you put it on paper and somehow by the end of the day you have nothing to show for it, been there and done that far too many times.

Within the story I referred to Compromise almost in a supporting role to the **Plan A**. At this point I would like to flip-flop and put the spotlight on *Compromise*. You must understand that Muststay College's need for a Plan A was because Compromise ruined the success they had built through planning and achieving. Compromise can be compared to the word *'Stress'* we know it exists and it is not good, but it is hard to recognize it before it does its damage, which is why it is referred to as the silent killer. Compromise works on the same order as it pertains to our dreams, goals and aspirations. For example, Muststay College had twenty-six years of an on-time graduation rate of 93% under the leadership of President Clarkston. Two things caused the decline in their graduation success rate, 1) They became complacent in their success and assumed they arrived at a pinnacle of academic achievement; and 2) They did not prepare for a replacement for President Clarkston, the visionary of the Plan A. They made the mistake many make in any successful organization that everything will always remain the same once success is achieved. This is a classic form of Compromise.

You run into Compromise when you stop doing the little things that brought you to your success, which is better known as the maintenance of your dream. What is important to understand is no matter how many people are involved in the dream and the Plan A; Compromise always begins at the head of the dream and trickles down. Think about organizations, committees, and businesses that have grown stagnant. Many times it's because ideas and directions have ceased to flow from the head of the dream. Here lies the decline of Muststay College, when President Clarkston resigned his position. Those who followed as President presented a Plan A but abandoned it to a backup plan as soon as challenges would occur.

Another danger involving Compromise is when people or an organization have never achieved much. Once they taste success they've never had, they stop to celebrate and take on the attitude, *"We have achieved our goal."* This may be true but there may be more to what you have already achieved. For example, the success you are experiencing could be 40%. You could literally walk away and leave another 60% of your success on the table. Finally, another evidence of Compromise is when the energy and drive that once fueled the dream and Plan A, gives way to laziness. Remember, it wasn't until President Getitdone and Muststay College put positive action behind their decision to be successful that things began to change. I hear the question that is in the minds of some, "How will I know if I am Compromising?" Well, I would like to recommend you check what I call the Compromise gauge. Whatever you are having success in, stop and ask yourself this question. "Have I experienced all the success out of this venture that is possible?" If you examine your situation honestly you will see the answer. However, more times than not the answer will be 'NO.' For the sake of your dream and Plan A, avoid Compromise.

Let's take a look at the star of our story Plan A; what is this? The Plan A I am talking about is really understanding your dream first. This is critical. Do you really have a dream to pursue and a goal to accomplish, or is it just the newest idea of the week which will serve as an Alka Seltzer tablet, fizz up and soon fizzle out? Plan A is based on a solid dream, this is why the Presidents after President Clarkston failed miserably until President Getitdone took over. Once you have crystallized your dream in your heart, mind and soul you then have a template to build a solid Plan A with flexible walls. Ahhhh! You noticed I said flexible walls, I never said you would not have to make adjustments to your Plan A or even modify it, I just said you should not abandon it. I hear my oppositional thinkers saying aren't you doing the same thing with a Plan B, C, D, E, or F? No you are not, and

LEAVE COMPROMISE *at Home*

here is why. When you adjust your Plan A or even modify it, you are using the same components you built the plan on. For example, a car company may have a Plan A to build a Zuzu car. Each year they may make adjustments to better the parts, interior, and the engine. They may even modify the body of the car every few years to keep it looking appealing; however, with all of the adjustments and modifications to the Plan A the design is still for a Zuzu car. The walls of the Plan A for the Zuzu car are flexible to make improvements or corrections. When you go to a Plan B, you have abandoned the idea of your original Plan A altogether. In essence, it has failed. Too many people plan for failure with a backup Plan B. If you go into your dream with a Plan B, what you are really saying is, "My dream might fail or only have a 50% chance of success." Why else would you go in with a Plan B?

When Muststay College re-captured their dream and Plan A, not only did they experience great success but like all quality dreams the success spilled over into the lives of others. The town of Pitiful became successful also and realized its potential. Your dream should affect more than just you. That is the gauge to tell if your dream is selfish or inclusive. Keep dreaming and build your Plan A.

"What if?" is waiting for you.

ABOUT THE AUTHOR

Reginald L. Hudson has been pastoring for 18 years, and is currently the Servant Pastor of the Union Baptist Church, New Rochelle, NY. He has been the Police Chaplain for Mount Kisco, NY for the past 18 years, and the Chaplain for the Department of Public Works of New Rochelle, NY for four years. During his 18 years of pastoring, teaching, and training, he developed a Two Year Certificate in Ministry course which met weekly for intense training and development. Over a ten year span, the course graduated five classes and many of those students are serving in ministry today as preachers, teachers, deacons, trustees, missionaries, and administrators.

In addition, Pastor Hudson has been privileged to preach internationally in Israel, Jamaica, Africa, and Brazil. He also hosted a cable television show for five years called 'Joy Hour of Power' and a radio broadcast entitled 'A Moment of Truth.' He is a graduate of New York Theological and Faith Seminary, Tacoma, WA where he is currently completing his Doctoral Degree in Strategic and Organizational Leadership. In addition, Pastor Hudson is an Adjunct Professor at Nyack College and Monroe College. Pastor Hudson is married to Shelly Hudson and together they have three beautiful children, Reggie II, Alexis, and Joaquin.

Any inquires concerning Conferences, Lectures, Workshops or Preaching engagements should be directed to **RLHudsonInc@aol.com**

To order additional copies of

Send Order to:
RL Hudson, Inc.
P.O. Box 483
Bedford Hills, NY 10507

www.ingramcontent.com/pod-product-compliance
Lightning Source LLC
LaVergne TN
LVHW051157080426
835508LV00021B/2672